PUNISHMENT: EARTH

CHOOSE FROM 15 ENDINGS!

BY R. A. MONTGOMERY

CHOOSECO

$6.99 U.S.
$7.99 CAN

ISBN: 978-1-933390-36-9

Kids love reading
Choose Your Own Adventure®!

"These books are like games. Sometimes the choice seems like it will solve everything, but you wonder if it's a trap."

Matt Harmon, age 11

"I think you'd call this a book for active readers, and I am definitely an active reader!"

Ava Kendrick, age 11

"You decide your own fate, but your fate is still a surprise."

Chun Tao Lin, age 10

"Come on in this book if you're crazy enough! One wrong move and you're a goner!"

Ben Curley, age 9

"You can read Choose Your Own Adventure books so many wonderful ways. You could go find your dog or follow a unicorn."

Celia Lawton, 11

**Ask your bookseller for books you have missed
or visit us at cyoa.com to collect them all.**

PUNISHMENT: EARTH

BY R. A. MONTGOMERY

ILLUSTRATED BY JASON MILLET
COVER ILLUSTRATED BY GABHOR UTOMO

CHOOSECO
WAITSFIELD, VERMONT

Punishment: Earth ©1988 R. A. Montgomery, Warren Vermont. All
Rights Reserved. Originally published as *Exiled to Earth.*

Artwork, design, and revised text ©2010 Chooseco LLC,
Waitsfield, Vermont. All Rights Reserved.

Cover artist: Gabhor Utomo
Interior artist: Jason Millet
Book design: Stacey Boyd, Big Eyedea Visual Design
Chooseco dragon logos designed by: Suzanne Nugent

For information regarding permission, write to:

CHOOSECO
P.O. Box 46
Waitsfield, Vermont 05673
www.cyoa.com

EAN: 978-1-933390-36-9
ISBN: 1-933390-36-0

Published simultaneously in the United States and Canada

Printed in the United States of America

0 9 8 7 6 5 4 3 2 1

Thanks to Richard & Leslie Gottlieb
for all your support.

BEWARE and WARNING!

This book is different from other books.

You and YOU ALONE are in charge of what happens in this story.

There are dangers, choices, adventures, and consequences. YOU must use all of your numerous talents and much of your enormous intelligence. The wrong decision could end in disaster—even death. But, don't despair. At anytime, YOU can go back and make another choice, alter the path of your story, and change its result.

As two of the youngest residents of the Planet Orca, you and your best friend Og are under the constant rule of the planet's elders. You haven't ever feared the wrath of the Supreme Orcan Senate, although you haven't ever strayed too far from the rules you've grown up knowing. When you stray into the off-limits Lost Region, you are surprised at what you find: a history of your planet you never knew about—even evidence of interplanetary warfare that must have occurred generations before your birth. On your planet, curiosity is forbidden and punished by exile—to an even more mysterious planet you know as Earth!

You and your best friend Og are in the Way Far Back, a patch of wilderness on the planet Orca. The environment on Orca is just like Earth's, but the Orcan civilization is much more advanced.

Even an advanced civilization can sometimes be dull, especially for a young Orcan like yourself. You and Og are feeling bored. So, despite warnings from the planet elders, you decide to explore the Way Far Back. Now you and Og are hiking in the direction of the Lost Region, a forbidden zone full of danger.

You reach the border of the Lost Region and choose to follow a path that's just barely visible under dense vegetation.

Turn to the next page.

2

After walking several minutes, you come to a swirling river.

"Should we swim it?" Og looks at you apprehensively.

"The current looks pretty strong," you say, staring into the water. "I've also heard rumors that some of the rivers in the Lost Region are infested with Orcan-eating green fish."

As you and Og consider the unappetizing possibility of becoming fish food, you realize that the walk has made you hungry. The mangoes hanging on the Juwawa trees look tasty, so you climb up to get some. While picking fruit from one of the highest branches, you and Og notice something mysterious in the distance.

Turn to the next page.

You see four black walls rising out of a clearing in the jungle. What are they? You and Og agree to hike in the direction of the black walls and explore the area.

Forty-five minutes later you find yourself standing in the clearing staring at the very walls you'd seen from the treetop. Up close, the black walls are even more mysterious and forbidding. From here, you and Og can clearly read the sign warning: "Trespassers Keep Out!" Still, you are curious and you've come a long way. You feel you must find out what's hidden behind the black walls.

Go on to the next page.

As you approach the nearest wall, you hear a rustling in the bushes. You turn quickly. Out of the bushes come three giant warthogs, running straight at you. You try to run back into the jungle, but your escape route is blocked by even more giant warthogs heading in your direction. You turn again and run back toward the black walls, looking for some way to escape.

Turn to the next page.

Og spots an old door with a large rusty lock. You pull on the door, but the lock holds fast. The giant warthogs are nearly upon you. They're so close you can see every hairy wart on their skins.

You pick up a rock and bash the lock, breaking it off. You yank open the door and pull it shut just in time to avoid being carved up by the warthogs' razor-like tusks.

After catching your breath, you walk through a short, rock-strewn tunnel that opens onto a sunlit courtyard.

"Look!" cries Og in astonishment.

At first the courtyard looks like an ordinary junkyard. As you focus, you see that the courtyard is filled with old space warships! They're scattered everywhere, here and there, as if they were nothing important!

Turn to page 9.

8

You secure your spacecraft to prevent anyone from entering it out of curiosity. (You know a lot about being curious, after all.) You and Og travel with a guide across the Chinese countryside. What contrasts you see! First you travel past poor farming villages on unpaved roads. Then, you continue on a wide paved road. Soon you approach a city that seems to be growing even as you pass by. The Chinese have a thriving society and you can easily sense their mood of great hope.

Finally, you arrive at a place you guess must be an ancient city. Its palaces and gardens immediately create a feeling of harmony and well-being.

"Welcome! We are glad that you came," a guide to the city tells you. "Our leaders will come to talk with you. They are very interested in hearing about your planet. You may stay here as our guests for as long as you wish. Stay in peace."

You and Og exchange glances. You know you'll stay as long as necessary, but then you plan to move on. There are many more governments on Earth, and now you're curious to meet with them all.

The End

War ended on Orca light-years ago, so the only space warships you've ever seen were those in your history books.

You and Og explore the old fort and the warships as Orca's sun sets in the east. You discover an old monolith overgrown with vegetation. You and Og clear it off and read the inscription: "Fort Triumphant."

"Isn't this the last of the space forts used to guard Orca from hostile enemies?" you ask Og, although you already know that from reading Orcan history. As more sophisticated defense systems were invented, the old forts became obsolete and were torn down. Fort Triumphant had been preserved as a monument to brave Orcans who had fought in the space wars. After light-years had passed, the elders felt that even the memory of those wars had faded. Eventually, Fort Triumphant, too, had been abandoned to rot in this Lost Region jungle.

Thrilled with your discovery of the fort and its artifacts, you decide to camp out in the fort overnight and explore it in the morning.

Turn to the next page.

10

The next morning, you and Og are awakened at dawn by a strange humming sound coming from one of the spaceships. The two of you approach the ship and cautiously step inside. In the cabin of the ship, the humming is even louder.

"This looks like an old-fashioned throttle lever," Og says. "On the old spaceships, you gained altitude by pulling on it." Og gives the throttle a light yank, and the spaceship quivers slightly.

Moments later the spaceship stops humming. "It must run on solar energy," you say. "When the sun shines on the solar pods, it activates the spaceship's systems." The now-familiar hum starts again. "The elders must have forgotten to deactivate it," you say as the humming grows louder.

Go on to the next page.

"Do you think it can still fly?" asks Og.

Funny, you've been wondering the exact same thing—and whether you should try to start the spaceship. After all, if you can't fly out of Fort Triumphant, you may have to face the giant warthogs again.

On the other hand, if the old ship does fly, it could break down in flight and come crashing back to Orca.

If you try to start the spaceship to fly out, turn to page 12.

If you try to leave Fort Triumphant the way you came in, turn to page 16.

12

After you and Og are secured in your seats, you pull back the throttle of the spaceship. The ship begins to rumble. Somehow it manages to lift off.

"Pull the throttle back farther! Let's zoom out of here!" Og yells.

"I don't want to give it too much juice," you shout over the rumble. "This thing's pretty old. I don't know if it can get to full power."

The ship starts to gain altitude. You hover over the fort and slowly begin to fly in the direction of the Way Far Back and civilization.

"Hey, this runs pretty smoothly for an old bucket of rust," you say as the spaceship glides over the trees toward the coast.

"It sure does," Og agrees. "Give it a little more power. Let's see what it can do!"

You push the throttle forward and the spaceship levels out and picks up speed. Within seconds you've passed Mach 1. You and Og howl with laughter.

Suddenly the ship starts to vibrate badly. The throttle barely responds when you pull on it. You lose altitude rapidly. Ahead you see the coastline and the sea. You and Og both yank on the throttle and desperately try to guide the spaceship back to land.

"We're not going to make it!" screams Og.

Turn to the next page.

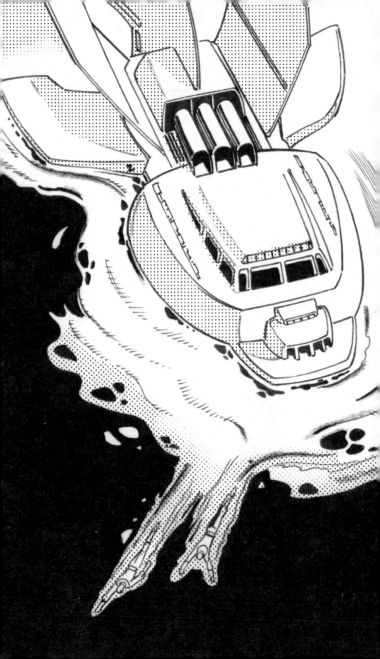

The ship skims the sea and comes to a stop right on top of the water. It's still in one piece, and so are you. But the spaceship is sinking rapidly. You and Og quickly escape and swim to shore.

The Orcan Coast Guard beach patrol is there waiting for you.

"We think you'd better come with us to see the elders," says the captain of the beach patrol.

You and Og know that the elders of the Supreme Orcan Senate will find out that you were trespassing in the forbidden zone. This could be real trouble. You console yourself by remembering that even the elders must have been young once. Is there any possibility they'll remember what it's like to have a chance for adventure?

If you try to make a run for it, turn to page 20.

If you decide to go with the beach patrol, turn to page 27.

Faced with this problem, you and Og leave the ship and close the hatch. You work your way back to the wooden door through which you first entered Fort Triumphant. Og cracks open the door hopefully and peers outside. Several giant warthogs immediately awaken at the sound. They jump up and wait for you to come through the door.

You and Og quickly gather up some of the loose rocks in the tunnel and begin to throw them at the warthogs. For some reason, the animals turn tail and run away.

"Those warthogs aren't so tough after all," you say to Og as the two of you walk out the door.

"They knew not to give us any trouble," replies Og confidently.

You are feeling good about your adventure when a soft rasping sound interrupts your thoughts. You turn to see a large lizard slithering rapidly in your direction. It has at least six legs and it looks about eight feet long.

Turn to page 42.

"Our chances of exploring Earth will probably be better if we just go unofficially," you say. "Okay with you, Og?"

Og hesitates, then agrees.

In a flash, it seems, you and Og are on an interplanetary spacecraft headed for Earth. You're the only life forms aboard.

"It'll be okay, Og. You'll see. We'll blend right in."

"Oh, sure. We'll blend right in, you say. Did you ever take a look at yourself in a mirror?"

"Come on, Og. Of course I have."

"Well, Earthlings aren't exactly walking around dressed in bright silver space suits with space helmets. At least not according to the pictures we have of them."

"You're right! I forgot."

"So, how are we going to blend in?"

"We'll fake it," you reply. "Besides, the elders must have foreseen this problem. Let's see what kind of costumes they've put aboard."

Turn to page 29.

18

"Oh, Venerable Ones," you say. "I do hereby fully relinquish my curiosity."

Og makes a similar speech.

The elders survey the two of you with benevolent smiles. They don't speak for several minutes. Then the oldest member addresses you.

"You speak, but I hear no conviction in your words," he says. "You are so young and have so much to learn. I believe that one day you will have much to give to Orcan society. You are brave, resourceful, and bright. A few years on the planet Earth will do you good."

"A few years . . . down there!" you say with a gasp. You exchange a look of disbelief with Og.

"It is not so very long," the elder says. "Who knows? Perhaps you two can be of use down there. The Earthlings certainly need help."

Turn to page 24.

You and Og are led out of the great hall and taken to a diplomatic courier vehicle. It's a large, silvery, bowl-shaped craft about the size of a typical Orcan house, or a football field on Earth. Rows of viewing ports encircle it.

You and Og are the only ones on board. The craft is preprogrammed. You'll be able to control the ultimate landing site once the craft is in the Earth's atmosphere, but any other attempt to alter the flight plan will destroy the craft.

Turn to page 40.

"Follow my lead," you mumble to Og, as you walk toward the LSAV-3—a small land-sea-air transport—parked up the beach. As you near the vehicle, you turn to the captain behind you.

"Excuse me, Captain," you say. "Is that a two-headed sand crab I see laying eggs on the front seat of your LSAV?"

You know that two-headed sand crabs are rare on Orca, and that your question will make the men curious. Sure enough, the captain and his men move right past you for a look.

When they do, you and Og take off running.

There's a sand dune just beyond a curve on the beach, and you just make it there without being seen. Moments later the beach patrol races past your hiding place looking for you. Trying not to laugh too loudly, you sit down to catch your breath.

You barely have time to appreciate your luck when you realize that you're being sucked into the sand. Your hiding place is a sand-crab trap! At the bottom of the trap, you imagine hundreds of many-headed sand crabs snapping at you with their claws!

You and Og yell for help and fight furiously to keep from falling deeper into the pit.

Fortunately the beach patrol is near enough to hear your screams. They rescue you just in time.

"You two mischief makers are going to see the elders whether you like it or not," says the captain, wiping the sweat from his brow. "And no more funny business or we'll toss you both right back into that pit."

Turn to page 27.

"Yes. I was in Fort Triumphant, Venerable One," you tell the Supreme Senate leader.

All the elders in the chamber gasp.

The leader shakes her head. Then she continues. "Were you alone?" she asks.

You don't want to lie, yet you don't want to involve Og in whatever punishment is in store for you.

"I'm waiting for your answer," the elder says.

If you protect Og, turn to page 35.

If you admit that Og was with you, turn to page 54.

"Can you make the nations stop fighting over Antarctica?" ask the men.

"We Orcans have had a peaceful planet for a long time," Og says. "What is the reason for the dispute?"

Antarctica is far from here and even more desolate than this valley," answers one of the men. "It is too cold for humans, but wondrous creatures live there. Seven nations have bases there. Many nations are fighting over the land. They want to study its uses. We fear they will ruin it," says one of the three.

His friend continues, "New Zealanders too have a base there. But we are desperate to preserve the

barren land for the penguins and other native animals. We wish only to protect Antarctica, just as we protect our sheep and our beautiful valley."

"Og," you ask, "is this a mission we can fulfill? Is this the reason we have come to Earth?"

Og looks happy. "I hope so, and I am very curious. Shall we stay a while and find out?"

"Yes," you say with enthusiasm. "How about a short trip to Scott Base? I'd like to see those wondrous animals."

But Og is already showing off the penguin images he has pulled up on the terra-shade monitors and is too busy to answer you.

The End

24

The elders don't know that you are actually excited by the idea of going to the planet Earth—the planet of curiosity. Your youth won't be wasted there, you think.

"Now, you two will be Orcan ambassadors," the leader of the Supreme Senate says. "I warn you, it will be no picnic. Many ambassadors have gone to Earth over the last thirteen thousand years."

"What happened to them?" you ask. "Did the Earthlings welcome them?"

"Not exactly," the leader replies.

You wonder what she means, but you know better than to let your curiosity show by asking.

"How are we to be introduced to Earth?" Og wants to know. "Who will the Earthlings believe us to be?"

"You can carry diplomatic documents and approach one of the major governments. Or," one of the senators explains, "if you wish you can go to Earth as what you are—young adventurers. You would be ambassadors in disguise, as it were."

You and Og briefly discuss your options.

If you want to be formally introduced to one of Earth's governments, turn to page 36.

If you want to go to Earth as an adventurer, turn to page 17.

"Let's go, Og," you say, activating the descender beam. "Everyone is here to greet us." A ray of soft purple light stretches from your ship to the ground. The crowd utters an amazed "Ohhh!"

You and Og begin your descent. But you never reach the ground.

Turn to page 57.

There's nothing left to do but accept your fate. On the way to the Senate building, you and Og tell each other that going before the elders is probably better than becoming lunch for crabs. You say that several times in the twenty long minutes it takes for the Captain to report to the elders.

"It's your turn, now," he says with a big smile when he returns.

You and Og stand at the doorway to the chamber of the elders. The entire Supreme Orcan Senate sits very still behind a huge table made of volcanic glass. The leader speaks.

"Enter!" she commands. You and Og walk silently into the room.

"We, the Supreme Senate, have heard that you two are slaves to your curiosity. As you have seen, curiosity can put you in real danger. Only if you agree to give up your curiosity and behave as normal Orcans behave will you be free to resume your lives in Orcan society."

You glance at Og. You know that Og is thinking the same thing you are. If you agree to give up your curiosity, you won't be able to visit the Way Far Back again. That seems like a lot to give up for one mistake.

But if you don't agree—what will happen?

*If you agree to give up your curiosity,
turn to page 18.*

*If you refuse to give up your curiosity,
turn to page 37.*

28

You are given an envelope with the official Orcan seal of peace and a round box containing a gift for the Earthlings. "Well, you're off now," one of the senators says. "Good luck, and don't worry too much about the ones who never came back. The Senate has confidence that you will succeed."

"The ones that never came back?" You and Og look at each other. What has your curiosity gotten you into this time, you wonder?

Turn to page 19.

You and Og disengage your seat restraints. You remember to check your instrument panel. It seems as if the atmospheric conditions inside the ship have adjusted to deep-space conditions, and you and Og can safely remove your space suits.

You see Og pull a pair of tera-shades from the pocket of the space suit. "What are you doing with those," you gasp. "You know you weren't supposed to take anything like that with you! Those are the most advanced wearable computer monitors we Orcans have. If you are caught with them—"

"Who is here to catch us?" Og asks. Not even waiting for an answer, Og puts on the tera-shades and goes to look for Earth wear. You have to admit those tera-shades look cool.

A quick search reveals a storage closet full of Earthling-style clothing. You look over the costumes from the many Earth cultures. "Oh, well, let's see what we look like." You and Og start trying on different articles of clothing.

Finally you decide on blue jeans and something called a T-shirt. The computer informs you that young people all over Earth wear this costume. You choose a shirt that says, "You went to Astroworld and all I got was this T-shirt," wondering what exactly that might mean.

As you close the storage closet, you spot a small, round box. You open it, and then hand it to Og. "Let's take this with us," you say. "It might come in handy as a gift to the Earthlings."

Turn to page 40.

30

As you settle down, Og checks the computer for information. In less than a second, the screen blinks.

ANIMAL FOUND ON EARTH, SPECIES FELIS. SMALLEST MEMBERS OF CAT FAMILY. HARMLESS AND GIVEN TO PLAY. CAUTION: LARGEST MEMBERS OF THE FELINE FAMILY CARNIVOROUS AND KNOWN TO ATTACK PREY USING WELL-DEVELOPED TEETH.

Just which size feline is in the E zone?

While you are worrying about this, a warning message blinks red on the display.

ALIEN LIFE-FORMS APPROACHING CRAFT. IMMEDIATE INSTRUCTIONS NEEDED TO ACTIVATE DEFENSES.

You are keying in your instructions when the computer malfunctions. In a surge of power, the spaceship leaves Earth without your command. You, Og, and an unknown feline are being projected into space once more. There's nothing you can do except wait—and hope you'll be rescued. You wonder if your supplies will last.

The End

Your spaceship hovers above the landing field as you and Og prepare to travel down via the descender beam.

When you reach Earth, you find yourselves facing a group of military people armed with archaic weapons. An officer steps forward, extending his hand in what is apparently a welcome signal.

Og grabs you by the arm. "Don't trust them! I've got a really bad feeling. Let's get out of here."

If you agree with Og's feeling, turn to page 43.

If you ignore Og's plea, turn to page 66.

"We accept your beautiful token of friendship," the Chinese leader says. "It is a good sign that you have chosen a crystal. We believe that the clarity of a crystal predicts the future."

The officer bows slightly, speaks to his aides, and then addresses you.

"China is an ancient culture. We have long recognized the changing seasons, the progress from childhood to old age, the rise and fall of nations. Perhaps you visitors can help this world pass its great cycles in peace."

"We'll try," you say, wondering just what you have gotten yourselves into.

Turn to page 8.

"No, I didn't enter the Lost Region," you lie. As you utter these words, images of Fort Triumphant flash through your mind. The abandoned space-ships and war artifacts still intrigue you.

Strangely, you no longer feel intimidated by the Supreme Senate. You take a deep breath. "No, that's not the truth," you say. Then you tell them the truth: that your curiosity led you to the abandoned fort. They listen in stony silence until you've finished.

"And you, Og. You went with your friend of your own free will?" asks one of the elders.

"Yes, Venerable One. I was as curious as my friend," Og admits.

The elders confer for a few minutes, and then the oldest member addresses you. "You are brave, resourceful, and bright. But we worry that your curiosity will prevent you from adjusting to normal Orcan life. We have therefore decided to send you both to the planet of curiosity—Earth."

Turn to page 24.

"Yes, I was alone," you say. "I didn't know that Fort Triumphant was forbidden or that it was in the Lost Region." You say this with difficulty, since you're not used to lying.

The Supreme Senate confers for several minutes. Then the leader speaks again. "Your body and mind are vessels for excessive curiosity. The best cure for you is a trip to the planet of curiosity."

You turn and look at your friend. Og seems about to speak. You shake your head, trying to warn Og to remain quiet.

But Og doesn't seem to understand you.

"I went there, too," Og shouts. "I went to Fort Triumphant!"

Turn to page 63.

36

"I guess it's better to be introduced to one of their governments," you say. "But why is there more than one government on Earth?"

There's a burst of laughter in the great hall.

"It is a young planet," the oldest elder tells you and Og. "Its people are fighting all the time. They do not trust each other, so be wary of whom you trust. Since they never agree on anything, one government is not enough. Even a hundred governments are not enough. Earth's political system is a haphazard mishmash.

"Unless you two set them straight, the Earthlings may blow themselves out of their universe."

Aha!—a mission of importance, you think to yourself. Your destiny. You risk asking another question.

"What are their problems? Isn't there enough food? Is it an impoverished planet? Is that their problem?"

"No. It is a planet rich in everything. There is enough, more than enough. They do not use wisely what they have and do not share. Earthlings often act like children squabbling over toys. Unfortunately, their toys can be deadly."

"I cannot give up n
I cannot stop brea
displeases you."

The leader of the S
and speaks in a fain
you so curious?"

"Aren't all young
"Has anyone led y
"No, no one."
"Have you been in
"You mean from
"Have you been r
"No, only what is
"Have you gone
Back?"

"Yes. With my fi
Back."

"And did you
Region?"

"Well . . ."

"It is simple. Yes
enter the Lost Regio

You glance at Og

If

If

Turn to page 28.

You're in scattered clouds, 26,000 feet above ground, when your ship is surrounded by Chinese fighter ships. You notice that they're old-fashioned crafts, with wings, but they still look powerful.

A voice barks through your communicator, "Identify yourselves. Repeat, identify yourselves."

"Friendlies," you transmit back on the same frequency. "Friends from the planet Orca in the Heraclean System."

More aircraft join the original fighters. They circle you in graceful, slow arcs.

"Follow us. Do not make any hostile or unplanned moves. We wish to believe you."

The descent through the clouds is brief, and you emerge over a rolling, treeless terrain dotted with small villages. It's agricultural land. The fighters direct you to a military base with a landing field.

"Looks okay to me," Og's voice is hopeful.

"Let's hope so," you reply uncertainly.

Turn to page 31.

As soon as your spacecraft travels beyond the pull of Orcan gravity, you get to work studying Earth history. You use the seatback computer terminal for your research. Og uses the smuggled tera-shades, now lighting up with zillions of data bytes. They really are cool, you think, as you see the computer data reflected in the lenses of the super shades. You feel suddenly proud of the Orcan engineers who designed them.

Og reminds you that you need to pick a landing site on Earth. You are amazed at the number of different places you have to choose from.

"How can we decide?" Og moans. "There are too many countries."

"Let's go for one of the biggest. Or the most powerful," you say.

"Okay," Og agrees. "This place called China looks pretty big. We could try landing there. Or how about the U.S.A.? It's something called a superpower," he says.

You have to decide quickly. Your uneventful voyage has been so swift you're about to enter Earth's atmosphere.

If you decide to land in China, turn to page 51.

If you decide to go to the U.S.A., turn to page 69.

42

"Run for it!" yells Og.

"Head for the trees," you cry as you and Og race each other to the nearest Juwawa tree.

You reach the tree inches ahead of the lizard and quickly climb up.

"I hope it's not a tree climber," you say to Og as the two of you reach the nearest branches. You and Og turn and look down. The lizard is lying by the roots of the tree with its tongue darting in and out and its yellow eyes blinking.

"I don't think it is," says Og. "But it doesn't look in a hurry to go anyplace else, either."

"Wait a minute," you remember something you read, "aren't those lizards vegetarian, I mean not carnivores, but herbivores, plant eaters. . . ."

The lizard seems to watch your every move.

"Big words for a guy up a tree," Og says with a laugh. "As I remember it," he continues, "there are lizards that are carnivorous, and lizards that aren't. If you want to hop down there and check out what this guy eats, you can easily satisfy your curiosity."

You didn't need a joke to remind you that curiosity seems to get you in trouble.

"No thanks, Og, I'll pass. If the lizard stays there, we're going to be stuck up here until the park rangers find us," you say to Og. "That is, of course, if the park rangers even patrol the Lost Region. I don't know if they do—that's not something I've ever been curious about," you add mournfully.

The End

"Okay. Let's go," you reply.

You signal your ship and are lifted up into the spacecraft by the ascender beam. The hatch closes immediately behind you.

Peering through a viewing port, you see a look of surprise on the face of the Chinese leader. He's stunned and he's still holding out his hand. The troops surrounding him are aiming their weapons at you.

"Hit the rapid-altitude button!" you yell.

Og presses the RAB. With a groan, the spacecraft soars away from this part of Earth. In seconds, you easily outdistance the Chinese fighter craft chasing you.

You and Og listen to the Chinese on your sound pod.

"What did we do wrong?" you hear the leader ask. "We offered them peace. Why didn't they trust us?"

When you hear that, you groan. "Og, we've made a big mistake," you say.

Turn to page 73.

44

You look around at this green, hilly place. "This will be wonderful," you think, "a great place for an Earth experience."

Og seems to be thinking the same thing. "These sheep are oddly attractive and not at all scary like that feline being we encountered," he says. "And these Earthlings are adventurers just like we are."

"Are you from the Scott Base? Is that what you mean by Orca?" one of the Earthlings asks.

"The Scott Base?" you repeat, confused. Og is scrambling to look that up via tera-shades.

"Scott Base—an exploration outpost created and manned by New Zealanders in Antarctica, one of two remote polar regions on Earth," he offers.

You have to decide whether to pretend to be from this place, whatever it is, or to say again that you and Og are aliens from Orca. How friendly are these humans and their animals? There are a lot of them, you calculate, many more than you and Og could handle if things go wrong. You feel lonely for Orca. You must decide.

If you decide to pass yourself off as a being from Scott Base, turn to page 72.

If you try to return to the spaceship, turn to page 95.

When your foot hits the pedal, the engine shuts down immediately. With the G-force no longer pinning you against your seat, you can reach the manual controls. You press buttons as quickly as you can, and Og hits the auxiliary power supply. The ship's nose slowly turns upward and the spaceship starts to climb.

When the ship is safely under control, you put it back on autopilot and let the computer set the course for Earth.

Turn to page 53.

As you draw closer to Washington, D.C., the airspace below you begins to fill with aircraft that you recognize as ancient fighter jets. You aim at a large open space next to a needle-like projection in the middle of the city. A quick search on Og's tera-shades tells you it's something called the Washington Monument.

With the push of a button on your computer console, you broadcast a message of friendship on all light and sound waves.

You descend to two hundred feet and stop. The air around you is cluttered with flying machines that look like bugs. The squadrons of winged aircraft fly above you. On the ground, hundreds of people dressed in uniforms are waiting for you.

Turn to page 25.

48

Your craft fills the sky and floods the ground with golden light. The crowd below gasps. Some run in terror, fleeing in small mobile vehicles. Others stay, waiting for you and Og to emerge from the spaceship.

Majestically, you and Og glide one hundred feet down the descender beam to the top of the pyramid.

The crowd utters a collective "Ohhh," as the two of you begin to descend the steep stairs of the pyramid. That's when you realize you forgot one thing. . . .

Turn to page 87.

50

You and Og control the spaceship as best you can as you guide it back to Orca.

"Let's head for the sea," you say. "If we crash into the water, we have a better chance to survive."

You manage to head the ship in the direction of the sea. As the spaceship loses power, it flies over the surface. Frantically you press several buttons on the control console. At the last second, the spaceship skims the surface, crashing through the waves. Finally the ship stops, still afloat.

This time, the sight of the Orcan Coast Guard makes you quite happy.

The End

"China it is," Og says, agreeing with your choice. "Just in time. We're entering Earth's atmosphere." Og fiddles with the directional navigator.

"China is a very old culture, at least in Earth terms," you offer.

"Big deal. It's old. What's that got to do with us?" Og asks.

"I think an older culture that's seen it all—wars, revolutions, success, famine—might be more receptive to our message."

"And just what is our message?" Og asks.

Turn to page 70.

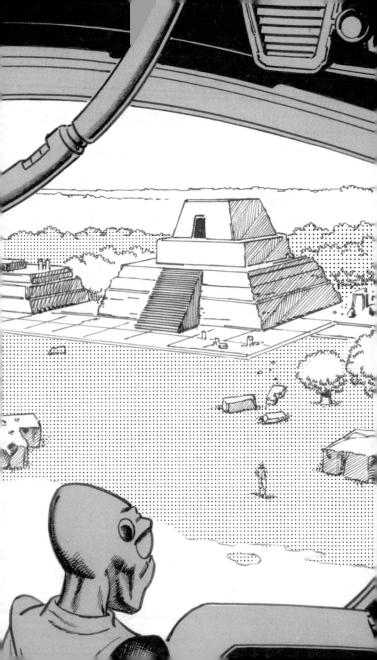

You are calmer by the time the ship enters Earth's atmosphere. Your spaceship descends in a slow arc, and then hovers above a beautiful stone pyramid in the midst of a scrubby jungle.

"This is Mexico," Og tells you, reading from the computer display. "And we're over one of the ancient pyramids of the Mayan people. It's called Chichen Itza. Shall we descend now, or wait for dark?"

If you want to descend immediately, turn to page 65.

If you want to wait for nightfall, turn to page 62.

"No, I wasn't alone," you finally blurt out. "Og was with me."

Og comes forward and takes your hand in a symbol of friendship.

"We didn't plan this," you tell the elders. "It simply happened. Curiosity isn't so bad. When you're curious, you wonder. When you wonder, you explore. When you explore, you discover. We're stronger for the experience."

The elders smile at you and Og with benign expressions on their faces.

"Your hearts are in the right place. Your bodies are not. Orca is an old and civilized society. We prefer to remain tranquil. We keep our young population to a minimum because young people are always so curious. Too much curiosity overexcites us, and we must guard against this. Yet, we understand your feelings; all of us were young once . . . many years ago."

The hushed chamber is hardly tranquil; rather it is electric with emotion. "For the good of us all, for the tranquility of our beloved Orca, you must travel to Earth. There you can satisfy this curiosity of yours. Stay there until your curiosity is satisfied! You might even do the Earthlings some good."

The leader of the Supreme Senate turns to you. "We could send you as official diplomats," she says, "but under the circumstances, I think an unofficial visit would be preferable."

Turn to page 17.

Aboard your ship the Earthlings are anxious but not frightened. There is a moment of awkward silence.

"Many of us on Earth have hoped for contact with life from another planet," the woman begins. "Things are happening so fast on our planet that we need your help." She pauses and looks at you and Og anxiously. "Can you help us?"

"We'll try," you respond together.

"Then, welcome," she says warmly.

"We're glad to be here," you say enthusiastically. "We're curious to learn more about your planet."

"I'm curious, too," says the young man. "Who are you?"

You and Og smile. "We're Orcans," you say. "I guess you could say we're the first Orcan ambassadors to Earth."

The End

56

"Have you ever seen one of these things before?" you ask, pointing to the spaceship and trying to change the subject.

"Must be one of those polar transport vehicles you have at the base. It looks really . . . new," the last of the three humans to speak says.

You just can't keep up. Base? Polar transport? What are these things? Anyway, your curiosity is starting to overwhelm your fear. After all, you and Og are adventurers, right?

"Actually, we are not from that place. We are ambassadors to Earth from the planet Orca. We have come to help you find peace."

Turn to page 22.

Some Earthlings in uniforms point long hollow metal objects at you. You hear popping sounds, and watch as small, sharp-pointed metal projectiles zip by.

You and Og smile at this strange method of greeting. Then, one of the sharp-pointed metal pieces slams into Og. He tumbles off the descender beam. Before you can react, three of the metal pieces strike you. As you crash to Earth, you hear a voice say, "I'm sure my bullets got both of them."

Bullets? What are bullets, you wonder with your usual curiosity. Your last question will go unanswered.

The End

58

Your spaceship begins its descent. According to the computer display, you'll land in a Tibetan settlement on the outskirts of a town in the kingdom of Nepal. The town is called Pokhara, and it sits at the foot of the Annapurna range of mountains.

You bring the spaceship down carefully, landing just beyond the courtyard of a Buddhist temple.

You and Og step out of the spaceship and listen.

"Om mane padme hum."

A man comes forward. He bows to you and Og, his hands clasped together, fingers pointing to his forehead.

Turn to page 101.

The woman and the crowd watch you silently.

You reach out your hand toward hers.

After a moment—she touches you.

You and the crowd are enveloped by a white aura. Everywhere, there is silence.

"Who are you?" you ask.

"Just me," she replies. "A believer."

"In what?" you ask.

"Hope," is her simple answer.

The strength of her belief convinces you that this ancient place is a good place to begin.

"Let's explore," you say. You and Og set off on your Earth adventure.

The End

"Night is better for Orcans. Let's wait," you say. "And we can get some sleep."

"Fine with me," Og agrees.

The spacecraft hovers unseen above the Earth as you sleep. You're asleep for only a few hours when your alarm system is activated.

Og jumps up and points out the viewing port. "The computer! It landed the spaceship while we were asleep."

Another alarm goes off, interrupting your thoughts. A life form is onboard your spacecraft and it's not Orcan!

Your spacecraft is equipped with a self-defense system. Should you activate it without even knowing what life form has intruded into your ship?

If you decide to wait, turn to page 71.

If you decide to activate the defense mechanism, turn to page 83.

The Supreme Senate huddles in conference. Then the leader speaks again. "You, Og, must go with your friend," she says. "The Senate wishes you both a fine trip. You may return to Orca when your curiosity has been sated."

The two of you are led out of the chamber and marched straight to the transit port. There you're given space suits—loose-fitting, comfortable, and functional—and put on a drone survey ship that is preparing for a close-range Earth reconnaissance mission.

Og smiles at you and gives you the traditional open-hand signal for good luck.

The craft is cleared for departure.

Turn to page 93.

64

"What's plan B?" you ask Og anxiously. "The computer isn't working."

"Return to Orca as fast as we can!" Og replies instantly.

"Not yet," you say.

In frustration you kick the computer. It rumbles, vibrates, and sparks to life. When its lights blink on, you activate the self-defense mechanism.

READY TO REPEL INVADERS. WHAT LEVEL OF FORCE IS REQUIRED?

"Medium force," you reply.

WHAT RADIUS?

If you want to limit the defensive force to just the spacecraft, turn to page 98.

If you consider extending the defensive force, turn to page 102.

"Let's descend now," you say. "I'm too curious to wait."

"Look at all those people down there," exclaims Og, pointing at the huge crowd gathered at the base of the pyramid.

Og uses the tera-shades to look up Mayan culture and reads the information to you. "Chichen Itza was the center of the Mayan culture, thousands of years ago. Earthlings still travel from all parts of their world to see these pyramids. They're curious, just as we are!"

"Let me see," you say, borrowing the glasses from Og. "The Mayans disappeared but they left behind this magnificent ceremonial site."

You and Og take turns admiring the huge pyramid of stone steps leading to a broad platform at the top.

"It also says that the Mayans predicted the arrival of beings from outer space. That's us!" Og declares proudly.

"Uh, Og," you interrupt your friend. "I don't think these particular people are expecting us," you say as you descend to within one hundred feet of the pyramid.

Turn to page 48.

66

"They won't hurt us, Og. Come on." You tug at your friend's sleeve.

"You go first," Og replies.

"All right." You walk forward, with your arm outstretched, and grasp the hand of the Chinese officer. "We are from the planet Orca, and we are happy to see you. Please accept this as a symbol of our friendship."

You reach into your pocket, but you don't find what you're looking for. You turn to Og and whisper frantically, "Where is the box? What did we do with the gift?"

"Oh, that." Og is relieved to find the box in a pocket and hands it to you. You open the box and remove an Orcan crystal. It's a little smaller than a baseball, perfect in shape and form.

"Take this crystal as a token of our friendship." You hand the crystal to the Chinese officer. "Orcans have watched your planet for centuries. Perhaps we can help in these dangerous times."

The officer stares at the crystal and then passes it around. You hear murmurs of awe and appreciation.

Turn to page 32.

68

You send a quick message to the onboard computer, and your spacecraft speeds into space to await your next command.

You and Og are aliens alone on Earth.

"I hope you know what you're doing," Og says.

"Not really," you reply.

You walk down the remaining steps until you're standing in front of the Earth woman.

Turn to page 61.

"The U.S.A.," you tell Og. "The computer says it's a young, aggressive, and idealistic country. But I've also heard it's always in trouble," you add.

"Maybe there are too many problems to solve at once," Og suggests.

"If you're ready, let's have a look."

You and Og guide your spacecraft to within a mile of the Earth's surface. You zigzag the U.S.A. at megasonic speed, from San Francisco to New York City, Detroit to Dallas.

"It looks a lot like Orca," Og comments.

"It does. I didn't expect that."

Finally, you end up over Washington, D.C. Your computer briefing pointed out Washington as the center of government.

You set your controls for a slow descent to Earth.

Turn to page 47.

70

That catches you unaware. Now that you think about it, you aren't really certain what the Supreme Orcan Senate wants you to achieve on Earth. Peace? Harmony? Can Orcans teach these things to others? Maybe time is all that Earthlings need to achieve peace and harmony. You wonder if Earth has enough time.

"I don't know, Og. I guess we'll just have to play it as it comes."

"Well, we'd better start playing pretty soon. We're in Chinese airspace and they seem to know it!" Og exclaims.

Turn to page 39.

You and Og wait quietly, watching the computer display. Suddenly, the computer pinpoints the location of the intruder. "ZONE E" flashes on the display.

"Let's go, Og," you say.

"Not me," Og answers. "You go. I'll stay here as backup in case you get into trouble."

You don't blame Og for being scared, but you need to know what's back in zone E.

With your courage rapidly fading, you leave the safety of the passenger zone and head for your fate.

Turn to page 105.

"Yes, yes, that's right, from Antarctica," you say, hoping you are saying that name right.

"What are you doing here then? Don't you mean to go up to Auckland to see the ministers? The annual Antarctica Wildlife survey is about to begin, and all the scientists are meeting in the capital," says a man who had been quiet before. As if on cue, the sheep start bleating loudly, to match the thumping in your heart.

"What are you doing here?"

You nervously glance at Og. But Og just shrugs. It's up to you.

Turn to page 56.

"What mistake?" Og asks.

"On Orca we're raised to trust and believe one another. Our way of life has allowed Orcans to advance. The elders told us that civilizations on Earth don't trust each other. We were not to automatically trust them."

"So?" Og says.

"The Chinese were trying to welcome us, and we didn't trust them. But if we don't trust them, why should they trust us?" You look at Og. He smiles back at you with understanding.

"All right," your friend says. "Let's try again someplace else. Where should we head?"

"Back to Orca. Being curious is not enough. We must learn a lot more about these Earthlings."

"And when we come back we'll give those Earthlings the benefit of the doubt," you say and turn toward the controls.

The End

You and Og wake up from what felt like a short nap to find that the computer has already landed the spaceship on Earth. But where on Earth are you?

UNS, your trusty Universal Navigation System, indicates you've landed in New Zealand. Og reads on the tera-shade lenses that this place is also called Aotearoa—land of the long white cloud—in a language called Maori. You ask Og to read more. He says this is a peaceful place.

Still you are cautious as you venture outside your spacecraft. Stretching and yawning, you sniff the air. It smells fresh and makes you feel instantly better. The gravity of Earth is a little less strong than that of Orca, but you'll adjust to it. The land is green and you can see for miles and miles.

"Strange place. No people around here," Og says while doing calisthenics to stretch cramped muscles.

Turn to page 81.

"The computer says Taos is an ancient village," Og tells you as your ship heads for New Mexico. "It's known for something called community living."

"I'm going to descend slowly, Og. We don't want to scare anyone. Turn on the generation 10,000 music pod. Let's listen to the chanting through our space suit speakers."

"Will do," Og replies, adjusting the sensitive sound-detection devices.

Through your clothing, the cabin of the spaceship fills with a rhythmic, pulsing vibration. You and Og begin to feel excited and reenergized.

"Hummm. Hummm. Hummm."

The spaceship descends slowly, glowing in the setting sun. Peering out the viewing ports, you see desert and mountains and a few winking lights from a town nestled in a valley.

Now you're one hundred feet above the chanting. You slow the descent, and the ship hovers in the air.

"I want to go and join them," Og says.

You nod and lower the spaceship gently to Earth.

You open the hatch and step out.

Turn to page 96.

You strain with all your strength to reach the manual controls, but the G-force is too powerful. When you relax, your arm slaps back on your chest as though your body were a magnet.

The spaceship levels off and then the nose points down. You're hurtling back to Orca! If you don't take fast action, you and Og will perish in a ball of fire.

You hear a voice coming through your helmet sound pod. Og is trying to tell you something, but your helmet is vibrating so violently that you can't understand the words. Og points frantically at your feet.

You look down and see a pedal. But what does it do?

If you step on the pedal, turn to page 45.

If you hesitate, trying to think of something else to do, turn to page 86.

You and Og pass the time reading adventure stories. After a while you both start craving some real-life adventures.

"Let's see what the computer has to say about our mission," you suggest.

You request information about your mission to Earth. You're astounded by what you find.

"I can't believe this," you say. "I thought we were being sent to Earth, but the computer has us programmed to land on Ocrania."

Turn to page 110.

Suddenly you're surrounded by hundreds of wooly four-legged creatures you have never seen before. They crowd around you bleating and making a racket. If this wasn't enough, the odors they emanate make you feel woozy. Despite that, they are kind of cute.

Og calls on those very handy tera-shades again for information. You really are glad to have those, even if the Orcan elders would be very angry if they knew.

"These are a life form called sheep that live in herds," Og says.

"Sheep?"

Just then you see three human beings rushing toward the herd that surrounds you. You quickly prepare to greet them.

"We come in peace from the planet Orca," you say. The men look pleased. The sheep are suddenly quiet.

Turn to page 44.

82

"We would feel more comfortable in our space-craft," you explain to the woman. "Would you like to see it, and speak to us there?"

"All right," she replies.

"Can I come, too?" asks a young man.

"Of course," Og replies.

"Anyone else care to come onboard?" you ask the crowd.

No one moves, and there's a mumbling of voices. Finally a man steps forward.

"My name's Becker. I'll go with you."

"Good. Follow us," you reply.

You and Og lead the way up the steps of the pyramid.

"They seem to trust us," Og whispers to you.

"Why shouldn't they?" you remark, as you activate the ascender beam, and the five of you are transported up to the spaceship.

Turn to page 55.

"We'll have to use force to get rid of the intruders," you say.

"Force can be useful, but it can also invite more force," Og points out.

"We'll just repel the intruders. We won't harm them."

"How do you know that? You've never done this before. You might use too much force," Og argues.

"It's a chance we must take, Og. We have to defend ourselves. And our ship."

Og turns away from you, mumbling Orcan phrases of discontent as you prepare to repel the invaders. You program the spacecraft computer for self-defense, but it doesn't respond.

Turn to page 64.

84

It doesn't take long for your ship to reach the Himalayan Mountains, a jagged range of snow-covered peaks that rises over five miles into the sky and runs almost two thousand miles from Afghanistan to the farthest reaches of India.

"Og, can you trace the chanting sound?" you ask.

"Yes, but not very easily. There are so many mountains in the way."

Your ship is cruising so low you can almost touch the tops of the gigantic mountains. They glisten in the morning sun, alluring and dangerous at the same time.

"Wait. Okay, I've got it," Og says.

Turn to page 58.

86

That pedal could be for anything, you think to yourself. Stepping on it might even eject you and Og into outer space. And that's the last thing you need.

But you've got to try something!

Suddenly, all is quiet. "The booster rockets must have shut down," Og says, breathing a sigh of relief. "We're running on the main engine again." Og gives you the thumbs-up sign.

"Let's not get too confident," you tell your friend. "We're not out of this yet."

Turn to page 94.

You and Og are surrounded by a visible field—a glowing mixture of white and orange light. You forgot to tone down your aura before leaving the ship, but it's too late now to do anything about it.

You walk halfway down the steps. "We bring peace and friendship," you quote from the phrase disk the elders gave you when you left Orca. "We have journeyed to reach you. We wish to be of help to your world."

The people stare at your aura, too hypnotized by its light to respond. You hope the elders knew what they were doing when they sent you and Og to Earth.

Og looks nervously at you, waiting for some response.

"Do not be afraid. We come on a mission of peace," you repeat.

A woman steps forward from the mass of people surrounding the base of the pyramid. "If you speak the truth, send away your spacecraft and meet with us."

If you do what she suggests, turn to page 68.

If you ask to meet with her onboard your spacecraft, turn to page 82.

Og gives you the thumbs-up sign and you both eject. You free-fall for as long as you can before pulling the ripcords on your parachutes.

Steam rises off your hot space suits as you descend through the cool Orcan atmosphere.

You and Og land with a jolt and are blown by the wind until you manage to cut the cords of your parachutes. You sit for a moment to catch your breath.

"I wonder where we are," you say to Og.

Og stands up and looks around. "You're not going to believe this. Look over there," Og says.

You get to your feet and look in the direction that Og is pointing. You and Og start laughing.

"Fort Triumphant!" you say in unison.

The End

90

Quickly you press buttons on the control console. The ship lurches left and narrowly misses the satellite. You set the spaceship on auto-control and head in the direction of Earth.

"We may as well try to get some sleep," Og says to you.

"I don't know if that's a good idea," you reply. "The way this spaceship is malfunctioning, I don't trust the computer to get us to Earth."

If you go to sleep, turn to page 75.

If you stay awake, turn to page 79.

You maneuver the ship, trying to position it so that the ship's docking arm can hook onto the approaching satellite. But you're traveling too fast.

You feel the jolt as your spaceship collides with the satellite and spins out of control.

You and Og fight to regain control, but the spinning is making you dizzy. You feel yourself starting to black out.

Will you remain conscious long enough to be able to reach the ship's auto-control button?

You feel Og's hand next to yours and together you're able to push the button. The ship's auto-control takes over and the spinning stops.

You look at the navigational indicator. Something is very wrong.

"According to the indicator, we're supposed to be heading into outer space," you say to Og. "But I can see the surface of Orca getting larger."

Og looks out a viewing port.

"Either the auto-navigator is still haywire or the satellite damaged the navigational equipment," you say. "We'll have to try and steer the spaceship manually. Again!"

Turn to page 106.

ARMING DEFENSIVE WEAPONS. READY AT YOUR SIGNAL.

You command, "Now!"

The computer relays a signal to the defensive weapons. A beam of energy designed to negate hostile action is sent out.

The beam is a soft purple ray of light that emits a low, rumbling hum. When viewed from a distance by inhabitants of Earth, the beam pulsates like a blinker or a signal light.

"Look!" says Og, standing at one of the viewing ports.

Turn to page 104.

You and Og check your space suits and engage your seat restraints. The space-traffic controller clears your craft for blastoff.

The spaceship takes off so quickly that you and Og are thrown back against your seats.

You look out the viewing ports and watch Orca, your home, slowly slip away. This is the first time either of you has gone beyond the atmosphere of Orca.

Suddenly the booster rockets kick in and the spaceship vibrates violently. A red warning light flashes on the control panel.

"What's wrong?" Og asks. You can see panic in your friend's eyes.

"I don't know," you respond as calmly as you can. You quickly spot the trouble: the auto-navigator has gone haywire. You'll have to pilot the spaceship manually or you'll crash back to Orca!

Turn to page 78.

94

With the G-force lessened, you and Og can reach the manual controls. You press buttons on the console, trying to get the spaceship to break out of Orca's gravitational pull. You manage to point the ship's nose upward, but without the booster rockets there's not enough power to escape the Orcan atmosphere.

"We'll have to reactivate the booster rockets," Og says.

"They've already used up a lot of fuel. What if we don't have enough left to make it all the way to Earth?" you argue. "We could get stranded in outer space."

"That's true," agrees Og. "What should we do?"

If you try to reactivate the booster rockets, turn to page 108.

If you try to get back to Orca, turn to page 50.

"Let's get back inside the ship," you whisper to Og.

You mumble something about equipment, and you and Og are back in the spaceship, leaving the bewildered herders and their sheep on the ground.

"Full power for liftoff," you say in as calm a voice as possible.

"Full power," Og confirms. Your spaceship rises upward in a smooth, noiseless path.

"Altitude three thousand feet and climbing," Og says. "Altitude ten thousand feet. Altitude thirty thousand feet and steady. What course?"

"Let's cruise around and observe a bit more," you answer. "I guess we are not quite ready for this ambassador job. It's hard to know who you can trust, even though Earthlings do seem quite pleasant."

Og adds, "The Orcan Elders knew something we didn't about going out into the cosmos."

Slowly orbiting the Earth, you pick up two readings that seem promising. From a place called Taos, in the state of New Mexico in the U.S.A., you pick up sound vibrations of music and chanting.

The other positive reading is from a mountain village in the Himalayan range. Similar chanting is coming from there.

If you decide to go to Taos, New Mexico, turn to page 76.

If you decide to descend in the Himalayas, turn to page 84.

A circle of people look at you as you step down. Their faces are open and trusting. You see no fear. Their eyes are welcoming. One Earthling comes forward. He's old, wrinkled, and stooped.

"Welcome," he says. "May Earth become your home. May these people become your people."

You take his hand in yours, feeling the love of the people for all things that move on Earth and in the cosmos, for the past, present, and future. You sense hope and joy in the people, and you feel it in yourself.

"Og, this is a better place than I expected," you say.

Og, shaking the old man's hand, nods in agreement.

"Perhaps there are other Orcans among us here." he adds happily. "Perhaps some who ventured before us found this place, too."

"Why not? Earth is more than a planet of curiosity," you reply, smiling. "It's a planet of hope as well."

The End

"Limit to spacecraft only," you answer.

ZONE ESTABLISHED. TIME OF ACTION REQUIRED?

"Wait!" you reply.

What life form is invading your territory? You want to imagine them—to use your higher Orcan mind to understand the alien life forms accurately.

But this time, no matter how hard you try, you can't bring an image into focus.

"Something is blocking me," you say to Og. "I can't get an image of this thing."

"You're blocking yourself with fear or anger," Og replies.

"Well, if you're so fearless, you try," you say.

"Okay," Og says confidently.

Turn to page 103.

"What's that, Og?" you ask.

"Sounds like visitors," he replies.

"Hey, let us in!" "We're friendly!" several voices call from outside the spaceship.

"Do we trust them?" Og asks you.

You hesitate. Danger may await you outside. But then your curiosity gets the better of you.

"There's only one way to find out," you say. "Open the hatch."

Turn to page 113.

"Namaste," the man says. "Welcome, I am Chodak. You have come at the right time. The world is in need of wisdom from other planets. You shall help us with our problems. You are welcome here."

Chodak claps his hands three times, and great horns, cymbals, and drums begin a ceremony of thanksgiving and welcome.

You and Og smile at each other. You know now you can be of great help to the planet Earth.

The End

102

You look at Og and ask, "How wide a radius should I request?" Earth now appears mysterious and foreboding. Your curiosity is slowly being over-powered by your fear of unknown Earth dangers.

Og shrugs. The decision is apparently yours to make.

You turn from the computer and begin to pace the craft.

"We Orcans are known for our fearlessness," encourages Og.

"But there's so little to fear on Orca," you reply. "No weapons, no violence. We must protect ourselves. Remember the other Orcans? Those like us who voyaged to Earth never to return?"

"Yes, that is a mystery still. I suppose we must protect ourselves." Og says.

You program a wide radius of self-defense methods and agree to the command prompt: ACTIVATE THE DEFENSIVE FORCE.

Turn to page 92.

Og gets into the proper mindset and goes to work. Og leans backward, muscles taut in concentration, head touching the floor.

"It must be a really strong mind at work. I'm blocked, too."

The computer blinks on: ALL ZONES NOW SAFE.

"What was it?" you wonder aloud, but before you can ask the computer, it shuts itself off.

"Well I'm exhausted," Og says. "This mindset business is hard."

You suggest that things on Earth will be clearer when its sun appears.

The two of you fall into a deep, dreamless sleep, almost a trance. Finally, you're wakened by a gentle knocking sound.

Turn to page 99.

104

The light and sound draw the Earthlings toward the spaceship. They are unarmed and calm. They're coming in peace.

Sunrise comes from the east, confusing you a bit. Orcans greet the sun from the west. This strange new dawn brings you and Og freedom from fear. You descend to a warm Earth welcome.

"Not bad," you say to Og, as a young child hands you a bunch of flowers and quickly kisses your cheek. "Who knows? Maybe we'll like this Earth so much we won't return to Orca, either." Thoughts of the other Orcan ambassadors fade as you consider the exploration ahead.

The End

The door to zone E is slightly ajar. Dim red lights illuminate the supplies that were put aboard the survey ship for you and Og.

You edge inside the bay, inching yourself forward slowly.

Why did you and Og agree to come to Earth again? you ask yourself.

A noise and a rush of air at your feet make clear that you are not alone. Some kind of creature is afoot. Right next to you, in fact. Its eyes gleam. It has sharp teeth. It stands on four legs.

You use only two to hurry back to the cabin.

Og asks, "Well, what was it?"

"Curiosity has its drawbacks," is all you can immediately say.

Turn to page 30.

106

You depress the manual control button and program commands into the computer. But your actions have no effect on the steering of the ship.

"I think more than just the navigational equipment got damaged," you say. "We can't even steer the ship."

"Looks like we're headed back to Orca," Og says.

The spaceship breaks back through Orca's atmosphere and plummets toward the planet's surface.

"It's getting pretty warm," Og says, tugging at his space suit. "Don't you think?"

"The protective shield must have been damaged, too," you answer.

"If it was," Og says nervously, "we'll never reach Orca alive. We'll burn to death!"

Turn to the next page.

The inside of the spaceship begins to get incredibly hot. Even through your protective space suits, you feel the intense, oven-like heat.

"I've got an idea," Og says. "Let's activate the emergency ejection seats and bail out."

"We can't eject now," you say. "The air's too thin up here. We won't be able to breathe." You feel the heat penetrating your space suit. In a few more minutes it will be unbearable.

"We can't wait much longer, either," says Og.

"You're right," you reply. "We'll have to take a chance and eject—and hope we have enough air in our suits to breath until we reach the surface."

Turn to page 89.

You press the button to reactivate the booster rockets. The ship's nose points upward. You call for full power and again the spaceship shudders. But this time it remains on course as it strains to break free of Orca's gravitational grip.

With one last shudder, the ship breaks through the Orcan atmosphere into outer space.

"That was a close one," you say to Og.

"I have a funny feeling it won't be the last close call we have on this trip," Og answers, pointing out a viewing port.

Looming in front of you is an Orcan satellite, and it's heading right for you!

"If we can hook up to the satellite, maybe we can be rescued," Og says quickly. "But then we'll never get to see Earth," Og adds with sadness.

*If you try to hook up to the satellite,
turn to page 91.*

*If you try to avoid hitting the satellite,
turn to page 90.*

110

"But Ocrania's barely habitable!" Og says.

"I thought it was only used to mine ore for Orca," you reply.

"Then that means"—Og looks at you in disbelief—"that we're being sent to Ocrania as miners."

"Slave labor is a better term for it," you say. "It's lucky we didn't go to sleep. Let's put the spaceship back on manual control and head for Earth."

"I hope the people of Earth are more trustworthy than the Orcan elders," Og says.

You and Og take over control of the spaceship and fly to Earth, where countless adventures await you on the planet of curiosity.

The End

Og opens the hatch door.

All around the pyramid and beyond, a large, silent crowd stares up at you. You take a deep breath. Then you and Og step out of the spaceship.

The crowd claps, cheers, and shouts "Welcome!"

You smile at Og. You're going to enjoy your time on Earth.

The End

ABOUT THE ARTISTS

Interior Artist: Jason Millet. Since graduating from Chicago's American Academy of Art, Jason Millet has created artwork for companies ranging from Disney® to Absolut®. His client list includes Warner Brothers®, Major League Baseball®, the Chicago Bulls®, and Hallmark®, among many others.

Cover Artist: Gabhor Utomo was born in Indonesia. He moved to California to pursue his passion in art. He received his degree from Academy of Art University in San Francisco in spring 2003. Since graduation, he's worked as a freelance illustrator and has illustrated a number of children's books. Gabhor lives with his wife, Dina, and his twin girls in San Francisco Bay Area.

ABOUT THE AUTHOR

R. A. MONTGOMERY has hiked in the Himalayas, climbed mountains in Europe, scuba-dived in Central America, and worked in Africa. He lives in France in the winter, travels frequently to Asia, and calls Vermont home. Montgomery graduated from Williams College and attended graduate school at Yale University and NYU. His interests include macro-economics, geo-politics, mythology, history, mystery novels, and music. He has two grown sons, a daughter-in-law, and two granddaughters. His wife, Shannon Gilligan, is an author and noted interactive game designer. Montgomery feels that the new generation of people under 15 is the most important asset in our world.

Visit us online at CYOA.com for games and other fun stuff, or to write to R. A. Montgomery!

ADVENTURER'S LOG

ADVENTURER'S LOG

ADVENTURER'S LOG

ADVENTURER'S LOG

ADVENTURER'S LOG

ADVENTURER'S LOG

ADVENTURER'S LOG

ADVENTURER'S LOG

ADVENTURER'S LOG

ADVENTURER'S LOG

ADVENTURER'S LOG

ADVENTURER'S LOG

ADVENTURER'S LOG

ADVENTURER'S LOG

ADVENTURER'S LOG

ADVENTURER'S LOG

ADVENTURER'S LOG

ADVENTURER'S LOG